SUIT YOURSELF

A Practical Guide to Men's Attire.

TIM MEEHAN

MY SALESPERSON IS

....

Published by J.T. Meehan Publishing
Copyright © 1999 Tim Meehan
Illustrations and Layout by Kenyon & Ami Ross
Photos used with permission from the following: Jos. A. Bank Clothiers, Cole-Haan
Shoes, Allen Edmonds Shoes, and photographers David Weiss & Larry McKay

ISBN: 0-9670738-0-4

Published in the United States of America

For orders or comments email us at ASTRAL61@ prodigy.net

PRINTED IN THE UNITED STATES OF AMERICA

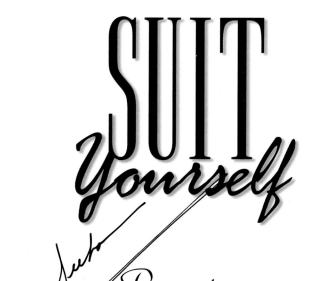

SUIT
Yourself

Presented to:

_____

By: _____

_____

_____

On: _____

_____

_____

Acknowledgments

There are many people without whose assistance and support
this book could not have been completed. The following is only
a partial list of those to whom I am grateful:

Jos. A. Bank Clothiers, for use of their clothing and catalog photography;
photographer David Weiss for use of the cover photo as well as the
still-life photography in Chapters 1-11 and Chapter 15 of the text;
Larry McKay of Cameras Brookwood for photography in Chapter 12-14
(also Michael Parece for set-up work on these photos); The Cole-Haan
Company for use of their shoes and photography (Chapter 7); and Bruce
Hubbs of R.R. Donnelly & Sons whose work in readying the book's
photographs for publication was invaluable.

Thanks also to Kenyon and Ami Ross for their outstanding
graphics, lay-out and artwork; Gayle Rudd for her assistance in
compiling the book's original draft; Chet Poczatek, master tailor,
who has taught me much of what I know about clothing;
Stephen McGhee for his input throughout and editing of the
final text; and Mike McCombs, whose suggestion that I write
a book on clothing set this process in motion.

Finally, a very special thanks to my friends, family, and customers
who encouraged me to see this project through to completion.

$\mathcal{P}$reface

Many people have questions about how to purchase and coordinate men's clothing. Though a good number are blessed with an eye for color, few have ever been instructed on the basics of dressing. Most of the people I encounter need additional guidance with their selections.

At the suggestion of friends and customers, I have written a short book which I believe provides that guidance. I hope the reader will find "SUIT YOURSELF" to be a concise, informative and useful aid in dressing for the business environment.

TABLE OF CONTENTS

CHAPTER 1
WHAT TO BUY & HOW TO START

Building a business wardrobe takes time. Few people can step out of college and into a clothing store with enough money to acquire a full wardrobe of business attire. This is true for most business professionals as well. Therefore, it is important for the purchaser of men's clothing to understand not only what suits and accessories make up the full wardrobe, but also which items should be his first priorities.

This chapter is divided into two sections. The first section lists the essential elements of the well-rounded wardrobe. The second section is a "Step By Step" chart outlining how to build a wardrobe in stages while covering all bases as efficiently as possible. The chart is primarily designed to help the buyer on a budget, but should also be useful for anyone wishing to 'fill in the blanks' of a larger wardrobe.

THE WELL ROUNDED WARDROBE

SUITS
Year-Round Suits
(100% Wool, Tropical Weights)

Navy Solid	THE
Navy Pinstripe	FOUR
Charcoal Solid	BASICS
Gray Pinstripe	

Black and White Glen Plaid	NEXT PURCHASES...
Charcoal Blue	

Charcoal Gray Glen Plaid
Black and White Mini Houndstooth
Tan Solid
Olives in Houndstooth or Plaids
Windowpanes in Navy or Gray

Summer/Spring Weights

Tan Poplin
Olive Poplin
Navy Poplin
Blue Pincord
Blue or Gray Seersucker

Fall/Winter Weights

Navy Flannel Pin, Plaid or Solid
Gray Flannel Pin, Plaid or Solid
Charcoal Herringbone (or Navy Herringbone Flannel)

The strongest recommendations here are "The Four Basics" in an all-wool tropical weight. These suits are extremely versatile and provide the wearer with a wide variety of coordinating options.

Button Down Collar   *Straight Collar*   *Tab Collar*   *Spread Collar*

SHIRTS

100% COTTON (Preferably Pinpoints)

6 White Button Downs
3 White Tab Collars
2 White Straight Collars
1 White Spread Collar
4 Blue Dress Shirts (any collar style)
1 Yellow Button Down
1 Ecru Button Down (ivory)
1 Pink Button Down
1 Burgundy Stripe
1 Blue Stripe
1 Black Stripe
2 Other Shirts of your choice (see discussion below)

This breakdown is not set in stone. Its intention is to avoid a stereotypical look with suits and sport coats (for instance, all button downs). Also, wearing different collars shows good taste, and by trying different collars, you may learn more about your own style preferences.

The striped shirts recommended here add variety to the wardrobe and will coordinate well with the vast majority of your suits and sport coats. The 'Other Shirts' mentioned above might include a 'Contrast Collar' (example:

white collar, blue shirt) or a Multi-Stripe (shirt with stripes that alternate in color). The French-cuff (requiring cuff links) is another alternative. This shirt is very dressy and lends a touch of sophistication to the overall look.

TIES

Ties are the most personal of all the business attire. For many men, choosing a tie often takes more time than choosing a suit.

Six to ten **red** or **burgundy** ties are recommended because these colors go well with dark business clothing. The tie patterns should be varied between stripes, paisleys, foulards, and modern.

The following tie colors are also recommended: **yellow, navy,** and **green.**

Yellow ties work well with most gray and navy suits, olive suits, and navy sport coats.

Navy ties are an excellent choice with Banker's Gray (light gray) suits, tan camel hair sport coats, and olive poplin suits. Many wear navy ties with navy suits and sport coats.

Green ties coordinate well with tan camel hair sport coats, navy suits, navy sport coats, and tan poplin suits.

Certainly there are many styles and colors available in neck-wear, but the above colors have been found to be the most versatile.

SPORT COATS

Navy Blazer- the essential sport coat
Tan Camel Hair sport coat
Gray Herringbone sport coat
Houndstooth sport coat
Plaid sport coat in blue, gray, or tan

DRESS BELTS

Black   best with navy and gray

Burgundy/   good with most colors;
Cordovan   best with navy, olive, or tan

Brown   possibly "mock croc" or gator belt;
                       works well with olive suits, tan suits,
                       and khakis

Note: Cloth or Woven leather belts should
                       not be worn with suits.

DRESS PANTS

Navy
Cambridge Gray (mid-gray)
Dress Tan
Charcoal (dark gray)
Olive tropical or Gabardine
Taupe

It is also recommended that you invest in some "fancies" of your choice. These would include houndstooth patterns and glen plaids. Purchase other colors (such as charcoal blue) to match specific sport coats.

HOSIERY / SOCKS

10 Black
6 Navy
6 Fancies (patterned socks)

In hosiery, wool/nylon and cotton/nylon blends in over-the-calf length are suggested. Merino wool socks are the best-wearing because they are soft like cotton yet more durable. When purchasing 'fancy' patterns, lean toward the navy/gray group to coordinate with the maximum number of suits.

POCKET SQUARES

Pocket squares (handkerchiefs worn in the breast pocket of a suit) are most often seen in 'higher' fashion markets such as New York, Los Angeles, and Chicago. The most common colors are white, burgundy, navy, and yellow. Pocket squares are used to tie the colors of the upper part of the outfit together and complement the overall look.

A STEP BY STEP PROCESS OF BUYING EVERYTHING YOU NEED,

THE FIRST STEP IS...

STEP	SUITS & BLAZERS	SHIRTS	PANTS
1	Charcoal Suit (100% wool tropical weight)	2 or 3 White 100% cotton pinpoint dress shirts	
2	Navy Blazer (First Sport Coat)		Cambridge Gray (medium gray) and Dress Tan (100% wool tropical weight)
	Buyers severely restricted by finances may want to opt for either the "suit route" or the "sport coat route." The "suit route" would consist of a charcoal suit, white shirt, tie, black socks, black belt, and black shoes. The "sport coat route" would be: navy blazer, white shirt, cambridge gray pants, black belt, black socks, and black shoes.		
3	Navy Pinstripe Suit (100% wool tropical weight)	2 more White shirts	
4	Gray Pinstripe Suit (100% wool tropical weight)	1 Blue shirt	
5	Second Sport Coat (from previous list of sport coats)		Charcoal Gray and Navy Solid (100% wool tropical weight)

WHAT TO BUY AND HOW TO START

CHAPTER 1

BELTS	SOCKS	TIES	SHOES
Black Leather (no thicker than 1¼")	2 Black	2 or 3 Red/Burgundy colored ties	Either a black captoe or wing tip (Allen-Edmonds, Johnston-Murphy, or Cole-Haan are recommended here)
Cordovan	2 Navy Blue		Cordovan tassel loafers possibly with a kiltie (the flap under the tassel-reminiscent of golf shoes)

NOTE: In Step 1, black shoes and a black belt are recommended. A cordovan (wine-colored) belt and cordovan shoes are also an option. In either case, the shoes should ALWAYS match the belt.

ONCE YOU'VE PURCHASED THE ABOVE, THE NEXT STEP IS...

	SOCKS	TIES	
	3 more Black socks	2 more Red/Burgundy	
	1 Navy, 1 Fancy (patterned dress sock)	1 Yellow 1 of any color	
Choose the sport coat based on the season - if early fall or winter, purchase the tan camel hair or gray herringbone. If spring or summer, purchase a lighter weight houndstooth or plaid.		MORE STEPS ON THE NEXT PAGE	

SUIT Yourself

THE NEXT STEP

AT THIS POINT, you have purchased three of the four basics in suits, two of the five basics in sport coats, and several of the pants, shirts, socks, ties, shoes, and belts you will need. By purchasing your clothing in this manner, you are achieving the most 'bang for

STEP	SUITS & BLAZERS	SHIRTS	PANTS
6	Navy Solid Suit (100% wool tropical weight)	1 more White	
7	Black & White plaid or houndstooth suit (100% wool tropical weight)	1 more Blue	
8	Another Sport Coat (from previous list)	1 Stripe in Blue, Burgundy, or Black	Olive and Taupe (100% wool tropical weight)
The fifth suit purchase listed here is the black and white plaid or the mini-houndstooth (Step 7). Either of these suit pants can be worn occasionally with a navy blazer, thus creating still another complete outfit. (A word of caution, however:			
9	Charcoal Blue Suit (100% wool tropical weight)	2 more White	
10	Tan Solid or Olive (Solid or Pattern) (100% wool tropical weight)	1 Ecru (goes with tan or olive)	
11	4th Sport Coat	1 Stripe	
12	Charcoal Gray Plaid Suit (100% wool tropical weight)	2 more White 1 more Blue	
13	Windowpane in Navy or Gray (100% wool tropical weight)	1 Yellow	
14	5th Sport Coat	1 Stripe (whatever color not previously purchased)	

WHAT TO BUY AND HOW TO START

CHAPTER 1

10

the buck.' Instead of purchasing individual outfits that require specific shirt and tie combinations, you have stayed within the Navy/Gray family of suits and sport coats, thus making most of your shirt and tie purchases interchangeable among your outfits. This is an efficient way to build a strong wardrobe.

BELTS	SOCKS	TIES	SHOES
Possibly a "Mock Croc" in brown or black	2 Black	2 Red/Burgundy	Possibly something in the brown family in a less formal shoe.
	1 Blue	1 Yellow	
	2 Fancies	2 (Your Choice)	
avoid wearing these suit pants too often with your sport coat, as this will wear out the suit pants prematurely). We have now covered all the basics in pants, belts, and shoes. Good Job!			
	2 more Black	2 more Red/ Burgundy	
	1 more Navy	1 Green (good with Tan suit)	
	2 more Fancies	1 Blue (good with Olive Suit), 2 of your choice	
	1 more Black	2 more Red or Burgundy	
	1 more Navy	1 more Yellow	
	1 more Fancy	3 of your choice	

You have now completed your purchases of sport coats, socks, and ties. The basic suit/shirt wardrobe is also for the most part complete. Simply review the lists at the beginning of the chapter for the few additional suits and shirts left to purchase.

Thus far, you have been asked to purchase only the tropical weight suits (no spring/summer weights or fall/winter weights). From a purchasing standpoint, the seasonal suits would be needed only **after** the tropical weights have been acquired because the seasonal suits are "climate specific," and thus less versatile than the tropicals.

Once, however, you have completed the chart as outlined, you may want to add suits from the earlier lists of spring/summer weights and fall/winter weights as the seasons dictate.

SUIT Yourself

CHAPTER 2
BASIC FABRICS & STYLES

HERRINGBONE

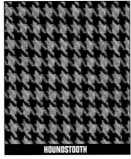
HOUNDSTOOTH

PINSTRIPE

CHALK STRIPE

GLEN PLAID

TICK WEAVE

WINDOW PANE

NAIL HEAD

BIRDSEYE

SUIT *yourself*

BASKET WEAVE

CAMEL HAIR

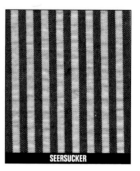

GABARDINE

PINCORD

POPLIN

SEERSUCKER

DONEGAL TWEED

CAVALRY TWILL

FLANNEL

WORSTED WOOL

MULTI-STRIPE

COTTON KHAKIS (CHINOS)

CORDUROY

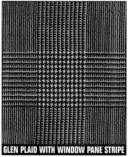

GLEN PLAID WITH WINDOW PANE STRIPE

CASHMERE

CHAPTER 2
BASIC FABRICS & STYLES

17

CHAPTER 3
BUY QUALITY

When buying clothing, you usually get what you pay for. Generally speaking, cheap suits won't last long, nor will they wear well or look good over time. Cheaper clothing may appear to be a bargain in the short run, but you will need to replace it much sooner.

100% WOOL VS. BLENDS

The most commonly recommended suits are 100% worsted wools. Many people, however, believe blends are better suits; a blend is a suit that combines two or three fabrics, such as polyester and wool, polyester and cotton, polyester and wool and nylon, etc. In this section, we will discuss the pros and cons for each.

100% wool suits generally wear longer, dry clean better, and last longer than blends. Blends, however, travel better with less wrinkling and are generally termed one-half ounce lighter in weight than all-wool (if a tropical weight wool suit has an ounce weight of seven to seven and one-half, the blend would usually have a weight some-where between six and one-half to seven).

All-wool tropicals, however, have a distinct advantage over the polyester suit - a polyester/wool blend is in effect a plastic/wool blend and plastic does not 'breathe.' **Breathe** is a term used when referring to natural fibers (cotton, wool, silk), meaning the fabric allows body heat out in the summer and retains it well in winter.

This is an important element in the overall comfort of the suit.

Furthermore, when you take a 100% wool suit to the cleaners, the cleaning fluids will 'take' to the wool fibers, giving a very uniform cleaning. Polyester fibers will not 'take' the fluids nearly as well; over time, these suits will develop a "sheen" in certain areas of the suit. The sheen usually occurs in the seat of the pants, the elbows, and in the front of the coat.

Finally, if you are relying on just a few suits for every day of the week, a new blended suit added to this mix can wear out quickly. If, however, you have a larger wardrobe of suits, there is less risk in purchasing a blended suit because you won't be relying on this suit to such a degree as to wear it out. This is a key point in assessing your own situation. If you are more heavily stocked in blends, the recommendation here is to purchase several good quality 100% worsted wool suits. These suits not only look great, but having them will extend the wearing life of the blends in your wardrobe. You can now wear the all-wools several days a week and rotate the blends in occasionally. In short, the blended suit will always serve you best as a secondary rather than a primary suit.

SUIT SEPARATES

A great innovation has taken place in the clothing industry over the past several years with the development of suit separates. There are now retailers offering men's suits in separate jackets and trousers. For example, you can now buy a 42 Long coat and select the appropriate size trousers to match the jacket. In years past, suits were available only in six-inch "drops" or "standard cuts." This meant that all suits made had a standard six-inch difference from jacket size to pant size. For example, a 40 Regular traditionally carried a 34 inch pant, a 42 Regular carried a 36 inch pant, and so on. Over the past ten years, particularly during the fitness boom, these six-inch drop suits were fitting a smaller segment of the market. The industry has at last adjusted and now accommodates a much larger segment of the market. Because of this innovation, the customer can now better target his specific sizes, making for fewer alterations and a more tailored fit without the tailored suit price.

CHAPTER 4
SUIT STYLES

The most popular suit styles have evolved in response to the variations in male body types as well as to style preferences. Your height, weight, and overall build should be taken into consideration when choosing which style is right for you.

JACKET STYLES IN SUITS AND SPORT COATS

1) Three-button coat – higher lapels, no front darting (or tapering). Very popular, this style is considered a classic look. The three-button is a good fit for men with broad chests and a fuller torso because of the high lapels and straighter cut of the coat.

2) Two-button coat – has longer lapels, front darts (tapering), and generally fits men who are slender and require some tapering in the body of the coat. The two-button is also a popular style.

23

3) Double-breasted coat – this style displays an overlapping effect in the front rather than the 'meet in the middle' button placement seen in the first two styles. This overlapping allows for alteration to the sides of the coat, creating a nice fit for the athletic build. Often the two- or three-button single breasted jackets have too much fabric at the waist to fit the athletically built man.

While these three jacket styles represent the more traditional look, there have been recent innovations in the cut of some jackets. Two- and three-button jackets are now sometimes cut with no center vent. Another departure from tradition has been the tapering of some three-button jackets.

Many businessmen have strong style preferences regarding their suit jackets. However, it is important to understand which style looks best for a particular physique. If you are tall, slender, and prefer a three-button coat, try a two-button the next time you visit a clothing store. Always consider the cut of the coat and make your assessment based on physique as well as personal preference.

CUFFS vs. PLAIN BOTTOMS

Generally speaking, go with cuffs on <u>suit pants</u> and <u>pleated dress slacks</u>.

For <u>khaki slacks</u>, the best looks are plain bottoms on plain front pants, and cuffs on pleated pants.

<u>Poplin pants</u> or <u>lightweight slacks</u> are best with plain bottoms (especially if you are wearing them to play golf- inevitably, cuffs fill with grass.

<u>Corduroys</u> do not generally hold cuffs well. The thick cloth will usually make the cuffs "wilt," so plain bottoms are recommended.

CHAPTER 5
HOW THE SUIT SHOULD FIT

In fitting a suit, a few points should be kept in mind:

- Fit the coat for the shoulders (the sleeves and body can be altered).

- Sleeve length should be in the joint of the wrist so shirt sleeves will show one-quarter to one-half inch beyond.

- The center vent (the slit in the back rear of the coat) should not separate. If the coat is ventless, there should be no tightness in the seat area of the jacket.

- The lapels of the coat should lay flat rather than bow out.

- There should be excess cloth under the back of each arm for forward arm movements.

- The jacket should button naturally in the front without tension from either side.

On the following pages in this chapter, we examine what distinguishes a good fit from a bad fit.

In this picture, the jacket is too small - the shoulders bulge beyond the true ends of the coat.

The center vent separates.

There is no excess cloth under the arms, thus arm movements are restricted.

In this picture, however, the shoulders fit properly (a straight line down the arm - no bulging at the shoulder).

This is an excellent fit, with excess cloth under the arms for forward mobility. The center vent lays properly with no separation.

Let's take another look at our examples...

First, the coat that doesn't fit:

Notice the lapels - they bow out instead of laying down naturally.

The shoulders are bulging past the natural end of the coat.

Also, there is tension in the middle. The coat wrinkles when it is buttoned and tugs from both sides - obviously too small.

NOW, Let's go back to the correctly fitted suit:

Here the shoulders stop at the natural end of this jacket. The line of the jacket moves straight across with the shoulders, and straight down with the arm.

Also, the lapels lay flat, the sign of a proper fit across the chest.

There is no tension in the front of the coat. This jacket buttons naturally with no tugging or wrinkling.

CHAPTER 5

HOW THE SUIT SHOULD FIT

With our correctly fitted suit, there may be minor adjustments to the sleeves or sides, or perhaps correction of a collar roll, but these alterations are easy to perform. (A collar roll is the line or lines that can form between the shoulder blades and under the neck, generally with men who have very square shoulders or erect posture).

An often misunderstood principle when fitting a suit is how long the skirt of the coat should hang for a proper fit. Practically everyone uses the "cup the fingers under the coat" method, but this provides only a rough estimate. The best way to know if a coat has the proper length is to run a tape measure from the base of the collar to the end of the skirt, hold that length and see if it is equal to the distance from the skirt to the floor. A properly fitting suit will measure close to an equivalent distance.

If the jacket measures too long, move from a Long to a Regular or from Regular to Short, etc. If you are between sizes, for instance Regular and Long, you should try on both, have them measured as described above, then choose the coat which best 'splits the distance.' If you happen to be truly between lengths, go with the coat that visually appeals to you. In most cases, a bit longer on the coat is preferable to shorter.

There is an important exception to this rule. Gentlemen who are stocky and shorter will sometimes do better with a Regular jacket instead of a Short to keep from giving the suit a "boxy" look. A Short may measure correctly, but could appear choppy. If so, choose the Regular length jacket.

BASIC SIZE CHART

Under 5' 8"	Short
5' 8" - 6' 0"	Regular
6' 0" - 6' 4"	Long
Over 6' 4"	Extra Long

CHAPTER 6
COORDINATING SHIRTS AND TIES

For those not gifted with the 'magic touch,' the coordinating of shirts and ties can be a frustrating task. Yet the basics of matching shirts with ties are simple:

- With solid shirts, know which tie <u>colors</u> look best.

- With striped shirts, know which tie <u>patterns</u> look best.

With a solid white shirt, for example, practically any pattern works on the tie because there are no lines on the shirt fighting the tie pattern. If we have a striped shirt, however, we need to recognize that the tie pattern should be spaced in such a way as to not 'get lost' in the shirt. The colors of the tie may be an appropriate match for the colors of the stripe, but if the tie pattern is too 'busy,' the overall look will be muddled.

In Figure 1 (above), you see a very complementary shirt/tie combination. The shirt and tie are seen distinctly and separately. One does not overpower the other, and the tie is not 'lost' in the shirt.

In Figure 2 (above), the tie has too much pattern for the shirt. Such a menagerie of colors and lines will greatly diminish the overall presentation.

This is a much better shirt/tie combination:

The pattern is somewhat spaced in the tie. This 'breaks the lines' in the shirt, allowing the stripe in the shirt and the pattern in the tie to complement each other rather than mix together.

This is a common error – a stripe tie with a striped shirt. This should be avoided. With so many lines moving in all directions, the look is better suited for a road map than an executive wardrobe.

This is an effective combination. The lines of the shirt and the pattern of the tie complement nicely.

An excellent combination:

Another overly busy look:

When selecting shirts and ties, keep these basic principles in mind, and you should have no problem successfully coordinating your look.

CHAPTER 7
COORDINATING SHOES, BELTS, & SOCKS

The discussion in this chapter is centered on a single statement: shoes and belts should match - socks should complement. For example, when wearing a charcoal suit, wear either a black belt with black shoes or a cordovan belt with cordovan shoes. The socks (hose) should generally match the color of the suit. Any secondary colors in the hose (as with patterned socks) should complement or match the tie colors. The hose (much like the tie) act to tie all the colors of the outfit together.

There are many kinds of coordinates when it comes to casual attire with belts, shoes, and socks. However, the business look calls for cohesion. An array of colors from head to toe will detract from the overall look.

A note here: in different parts of the country, fashions in business attire will inevitably vary. In the 'higher' fashion markets (Los Angeles, New York City, etc.) the "contrast look" with hosiery is acceptable. This is simply contrasting the hose with the suit (charcoal suit with tan socks, etc.). Whether you prefer the contrast look with your dress hose, or the complementary look we have recommended here, work from the base color of the suit and the tie to derive your particular look in hosiery.

CHAPTER 8
MATCHING COLORS

The keys to matching colors are to work around your 'base color' and to understand what works best with that particular color.

'Base color' refers to the dominant color in the suit or sport coat. By learning which colors best complement a given 'base color,' the business executive can not only improve the overall look of his wardrobe, but can also create an almost unlimited number of combinations from just a few suits.

The CHART OF COLORS on the following pages diagrams a number of effective shirt and tie combinations for the most commonly worn suits. The chart is designed as a reference guide to be used any time the reader has questions regarding a particular combination.

CHART OF

SUIT COLOR	SHIRTS	GOOD TIE COLORS WITH THIS SHIRT
Navy Solid	White	Red, Burgundy, Green
	Blue	Yellow, Gold
	Yellow	Bright Red, Kelly Green
	Pink	Burgundy, Navy (if you prefer matching the color versus contrasting it)
	Blue Stripe	Yellow, Burgundy, Red, Green
	Burgundy Stripe	Yellow, Burgundy, Navy (if you prefer matching the color versus contrasting it)
Navy Pinstripe	White	Red, Burgundy, Green
	Blue	Yellow, Gold
	Yellow	Bright Red, Kelly Green
	Pink	Burgundy, Navy (if you prefer matching the color versus contrasting it)
Charcoal Blue Solid	White	Red, Burgundy, Green
	Blue	Yellow, Gold
	Yellow	Bright Red, Kelly Green
	Pink	Burgundy, Navy (if you prefer matching the color versus contrasting it)
	Blue Stripe	Yellow, Burgundy, Red, Green
	Burgundy Stripe	Yellow, Burgundy, Navy (if you prefer matching the color versus contrasting it)

COLORS

SUIT
Yourself

SUIT COLOR	SHIRTS	GOOD TIE COLORS WITH THIS SHIRT
Charcoal Blue with either a Pinstripe, Plaid, or Windowpane	White	Red, Burgundy, Green
	Blue	Yellow, Gold
	Yellow	Bright Red, Kelly Green
	Pink	Burgundy, Navy (if you prefer matching the color versus contrasting it)
Charcoal Gray Solid	White	Red, Burgundy, Green
	Blue	Yellow, Gold
	Yellow	Bright Red, Kelly Green
	Pink	Burgundy, Black (if you prefer matching the color versus contrasting it)
	Black Stripe	Yellow, Burgundy, Red, Green
	Burgundy Stripe	Yellow, Burgundy, Black (if you prefer matching the color vs contrasting it)
Gray Pinstripe	White	Red, Burgundy, Green, Navy
	Blue	Yellow, Gold
	Yellow	Bright Red, Kelly Green
	Pink	Burgundy, Black
	NOTE	If the suit is dark gray, delete the navy tie. If the suit is not quite as dark, delete the green ties.
Black & White Glen Plaid	White	Red, Burgundy, Navy, Yellow, Black
	Yellow	Bright Red, Navy
	Pink	Burgundy, Navy, Black
Black & White Mini Houndstooth	White	Red, Burgundy, Navy, Yellow, Black
	Blue	Yellow, Gold

SUIT COLOR	SHIRTS	GOOD TIE COLORS WITH THIS SHIRT
Black & White Mini Houndstooth (continued)	Pink	Burgundy, Black
	Yellow	Bright Red
Tan Solid	White	Red, Burgundy, Navy, Green, Yellow
	Blue	Yellow
	Ecru	Green, Olive, Burgundy, Navy, Black
	Yellow	Green, Bright Red, Navy
	Burgundy Stripe	Burgundy, Navy, Yellow
	Blue Stripe	Red, Burgundy, Yellow
	Black Stripe	Red, Burgundy, Yellow, Black
	Green Stripe	Red, Burgundy, Navy, Yellow

SUIT COLOR	SHIRTS	GOOD TIE COLORS WITH THIS SHIRT
Olive Solid	White	Red, Burgundy, Yellow, Navy
	Ecru	Red, Burgundy, Navy, Black
	Yellow	Bright Red, Navy
	Blue	Yellow
	Burgundy Stripe	Burgundy, Navy, Yellow
	Blue Stripe	Red, Burgundy, Yellow
	Black Stripe	Red, Burgundy, Yellow, Black
Olive Pattern (Houndstooth Plaid, Windowpane or Pinstripe)	White	Red, Burgundy, Yellow, Navy
	Ecru	Red, Burgundy, Navy, Black
	Yellow	Bright Red, Navy
	Blue	Yellow

CHAPTER 8
MATCHING COLORS

CHAPTER 9
HOW TO TIE A TIE

EXAMPLE 1
FOUR-IN-HAND

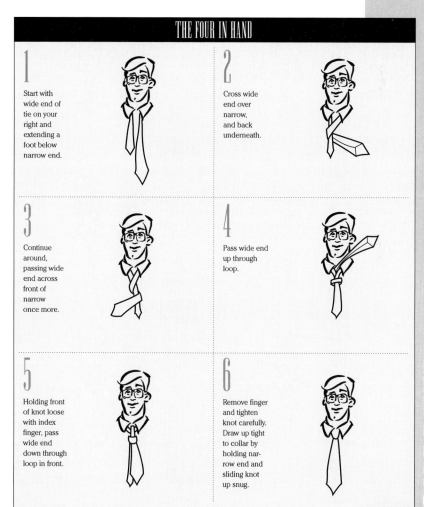

THE FOUR IN HAND

1 Start with wide end of tie on your right and extending a foot below narrow end.

2 Cross wide end over narrow, and back underneath.

3 Continue around, passing wide end across front of narrow once more.

4 Pass wide end up through loop.

5 Holding front of knot loose with index finger, pass wide end down through loop in front.

6 Remove finger and tighten knot carefully. Draw up tight to collar by holding narrow end and sliding knot up snug.

EXAMPLE 2

HALF-WINDSOR

HALF-WINDSOR

1 Start with wide end of tie on your right and extending a foot below narrow end.

2 Cross wide end over narrow, and back underneath.

3 Continue around, passing wide end back through the loop.

4 Now bring the wide end back over the narrow end.

5 Once more bring the wide end up through the loop.

6 Bring the wide end down through the outer loop in front. Tighten the knot using both hands.

EXAMPLE 3
FULL-WINDSOR

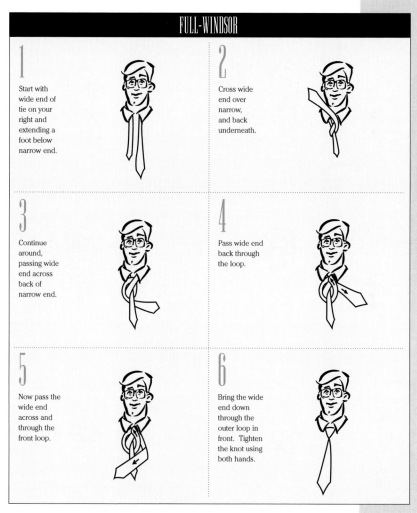

FULL-WINDSOR

1
Start with wide end of tie on your right and extending a foot below narrow end.

2
Cross wide end over narrow, and back underneath.

3
Continue around, passing wide end across back of narrow end.

4
Pass wide end back through the loop.

5
Now pass the wide end across and through the front loop.

6
Bring the wide end down through the outer loop in front. Tighten the knot using both hands.

EXAMPLE 4
THE BOW TIE

THE BOW TIE

1
Start with end in left hand extending one and one-half inches below that in right hand.

2
Cross longer end over shorter and pass up through loop.

3
Form front loop of bow by doubling up shorter end (hanging) and placing across collar points.

4
Hold this front loop with thumb and forefinger of left hand. Drop long end down over front.

5
Place right forefinger, pointing up, on bottom half of hanging end. Pass up behind front loop and...

6
Push resulting loop through knot behind front loop (see illustration). Even ends and tighten.

CHAPTER 9
HOW TO TIE A TIE

CHAPTER 10
DO'S & DON'TS

DON'T wear a navy suit coat as a navy blazer

✗ DON'T wear a navy blazer with navy suit pants

✗ DON'T wear a collar bar with a button-down shirt

✗ DON'T wear a button-down shirt with a double-breasted suit or sport coat

✗ DON'T wear a casual belt with a business suit

✗ DON'T wear striped shirts with striped suits

✗ DON'T wear clip-on ties

✗ DON'T wear short-sleeve dress shirts with a suit

✗ DON'T wear suspenders and a belt

SUIT *yourself*

✗ DON'T mix and match suit tops and bottoms

✗ DON'T wear clip-on suspenders, wear suspenders that button

✗ DON'T dry clean your suits more than twice a season

✗ DON'T over-wear your suits

✗ DON'T wear striped shirts with pinstripe suits

✗ DON'T wear striped shirts with glen plaid suits

✗ DON'T wear excessive jewelry on the wrists and hands

CHAPTER 10
DO'S AND DON'TS

- ✔ DO wear a tab collar, straight collar, or spread collar with a double-breasted sport coat or suit

- ✔ DO wear over-the-calf socks with suits

- ✔ DO wear t-shirts with dress shirts

- ✔ DO cuff suit pants

- ✔ DO use the "four-in-hand" knot for ties

- ✔ DO wear suspenders or a belt

- ✔ DO rotate wearing suits and also rotate sport coat, slack combinations

- ✔ DO wear belts that match your shoe color

- ✔ DO use shoe trees in your dress shoes

CHAPTER 11
DRESSING FOR THE INTERVIEW

When dressing for the interview, keep your clothing understated but classic. Remember, you want to do the talking, not your suit.

The best suit choices for the interview will generally be the "four basics" listed in Chapter 1: the charcoal solid, navy solid, gray pinstripe, and navy pinstripe. These suits have been around forever and will continue to be a mainstay in the wardrobe. The temptation to impress the prospective employer with bolder attire should (in most cases) be resisted.

Those who avoid the four basics in choosing the interview suit tend to create hit-or-miss situations in which employers are either greatly impressed or instead put off by the interview subject's choice in attire. The old adage 'better safe than sorry' applies here; a great suit selection won't win the job, but a bad suit selection could lose it.

Furthermore, with any of the four basics, your look will be both classic and understated, conveying intelligence, professionalism, and, not to be taken lightly, a knowledge of how to dress. This is important to a prospective employer because, if hired, you will represent his company. Whether you work in-house or in the field, your appearance will be a reflection of his judgment and that of his firm. Therefore, your appearance at the interview should not only be professional, but also reassuring to the employer.

Because first impressions are generally formed within ten to eighteen seconds, it is imperative to have strong non-verbal communication (attire, facial expressions, posture) at the interview. Simply put, no one can say enough about themselves in ten or eighteen seconds to land a position. However, positive non-verbal communication, coupled with solid verbal skills, will signal the potential employer that you not only look the part, but also have the potential to become a valued employee.

CHAPTER 12
"CASUAL DAY" DEFINED

Casual Days at work are becoming more commonplace. This chapter is designed to aid employers and employees alike in regard to casual dress. Casual Days are an excellent way to improve employee morale, yet many are unsure as to the meaning of "casual dressing."

There are three types of casual attire:

1) Dress Casual
2) Corporate Casual
3) Active Casual

The following pages contain several illustrations of these three variants of casual dress.

"DRESS CASUAL" Examples

1. Blazer / Sport Coat
   Tie
   Dress Slacks
   Dress Belt
   Kiltie Loafers / Loafers / Semi-Dress Lace-ups

2. Sport Coat
   Tie
   Khakis / Olive / Oyster Pants
   (in cotton or wool)
   Kiltie Loafers / Loafers / Semi-Dress Lace-ups

3. Blazer
   Button Down Shirt
   Dress Slacks
   Kiltie Loafers / Loafers / Semi-Dress Lace-ups

"CORPORATE CASUAL" Examples

1. Blazer / Sport Coat
   Tie (Optional)
   Dress Slacks
   Dress Belt
   Kiltie Loafers / Loafers / Semi-Dress Lace-ups

2. Sport Coat
   Tie (Optional)
   Khakis / Olive / Oyster Pants
   (in cotton or wool)
   Kiltie Loafers / Loafers / Semi-Dress Lace-ups

3. Blazer
   Button Down Shirt
   Dress Slacks
   Kiltie Loafers / Loafers / Semi-Dress Lace-ups

SUIT
Yourself

"ACTIVE CASUAL" Examples

1. Polo Style Shirts
   Khaki, Olive, Oyster & Navy
     Cotton Pants
   Dress slacks in wool or wool blends

2. Sport long or short sleeve
   Collared shirts
   Khaki, Olive, Oyster or wool blends

3. Polo Style Shirts
   Vests
   Cotton Khakis
   Sport Shirts
   Cotton Shorts (if company approves)

NOTE: "Active Casual" is essentially the equivalent of the attire one would associate with the golfers and spectators at a professional event.

TIPS for purchasing and wearing casual clothes

- Three pairs of khaki cotton slacks are suggested.
  These are versatile and a staple in casual attire.

- Buy sport shirts with the idea of wearing a tie with them
  to dress up your casual look.

- Try blazers other than navy if your company requires
  more of a "Dress Casual" look. The purchase of an
  additional blazer or two will provide greater versatility
  with casual shirts and slacks.

- As discussed in Chapter 3, buying quality is always the
  best course. This is particularly important with casual
  wear, because cotton khakis, shorts, and polo style
  shirts must be able to endure repeated machine
  washings. Quality purchases will yield great dividends
  in the long run.

CHAPTER 13

OUTERWEAR

The term 'business outerwear' refers to trench coats and topcoats. Both are popular choices for the business setting. This chapter briefly examines the popular styles in each type of coat.

TRENCH COATS

The most traditional trench coats are the double-breasted and single-breasted in tan and olive. Trench coats generally have a zip-out lining and are worn year-round. In the fall and winter, these are commonly worn with the liner for warmth. In the spring and summer, trench coats can be worn as a raincoat without the liner, as the outer shells of these coats are lightweight and generally rain-repellent.

Single-Breasted Trench Coat

Double-Breasted Trench Coat

CHAPTER 13

OUTERWEAR

65

Black Double-Breasted Topcoat   Charcoal Single-Breasted Topcoat   Navy Single-Breasted Topcoat

TOPCOATS

Topcoats provide a more formal look and are commonly worn in colder climates. These coats are most often made of 100% wool, 100% cashmere or a blend of the two. The most common colors are navy, charcoal, and black in single- and double-breasted. A more fashion-oriented topcoat is the British tan, but this style is less commonly seen.

SUIT
Yourself

CHAPTER 14
FORMAL WEAR

The Black Tailcoat with white pique vest and white bow tie is the most formal of evening wear styles and is most commonly seen at balls, galas, and other "white tie" affairs.

More appropriate for "black tie" occasions such as weddings and formal dances are the Shawl Collar, Notch Lapel, Peak Lapel, and Double-Breasted (all pictured here).

SHAWL COLLAR

The Shawl Collar offers a rather formal look; the Shawl traces its lineage to the Smoking Jacket.

NOTCH COLLAR

The Notch Lapel has a 'suit-interpreted' jacket style—the look is a stylized derivative of the single-breasted suit coat.

SUIT
Yourself

PEAK LAPEL

The Peak Lapel provides a very formal look, and is in fact a direct descendant of the Tailcoat.

DOUBLE BREASTED

The Double-Breasted model, like the Notch Collar, is suit-interpreted. This is also a popular style.

OTHER TUXEDO ACCESSORIES

Shirt (wing or straight collar), Bow Tie (either pre-tied or untied), Cummerbund, Stud Set, Vest (optional), Braces (optional).

During holidays or other festive occasions, colorful cummerbund-and-tie sets often add excellent character to the tuxedo while still providing the wearer with an appealing formal look.

The patent-leather bow shoe is the most formal tuxedo shoe.

PATENT BOW

THE PATENT LEATHER LACE-UP is also a popular choice.

NOTE: If tuxedo shoes are unavailable, the black cap-toe lace-up would serve as the best acceptable substitute.

CHAPTER 15

HELPFUL HINTS WHEN BUYING FOR MEN

Obviously, when you are buying something for someone other than yourself, taste can become an issue.

Yet the key to making good wardrobe selections for men is to recognize that the individual components of the wardrobe are not as important as the coordination of these components (see Chapter 8 - "Matching Colors"). Many a beautiful tie may never leave the closet for want of an appropriate shirt-and-suit combination.

What follows are several tips you may want to consider when purchasing clothes for the men in your life:

- Develop a relationship with a sales consultant at your favorite men's store. Have your consultant keep a record of your purchases, including sizes and styles. You can also maintain your own size charts and purchase history by utilizing the specially designed Size Charts located in the back of this book. Such records will enhance your ability to coordinate purchases over the long term.

- Ask your consultant about upcoming sales events and new arrivals. The amount of inventory varies throughout the year; selection is much greater when stock levels are at their peak.

- Purchase items which both complement and coordinate with the suits, shirts, and ties he already owns. Just a few well-placed purchases can greatly increase the number of combinations available in his wardrobe.

- Finally, in regard to their clothing, men are generally creatures of habit. His refusal to part with his now-threadbare Gray Pinstripe suit tells us there is no safer purchase for him than a new Gray Pinstripe suit.

TIM'S QUICK REFERENCE GUIDE

Below are HIS and HER cut-out guides outlining the
statistical information necessary to make efficient clothing
purchases. These cut-outs should save time and
eliminate unnecessary returns.

Tim's Quick Reference Cut-Outs (His for Wallet)

e_____

_____ Pants W-___L-____ Shirt _____ Belt _____

es _____ Polo _____ Shorts _____ Und Wear _____

EFER

☐ Pleated Pants	☐ Plain Pants	☐ Cuffs
☐ Plain Bottoms	☐ 2 Button	☐ 3 Button
☐ Dbl Breast Suits	☐ Button Downs	☐ Str Coll.
☐ Spread Coll.	☐ O.T. Calf Socks	☐ Mid Calf Socks
☐ Conserv. Ties	☐ Mod. Conserv.	☐ No Preference

ments: _____

Tim's Quick Reference Cut-Outs (Hers for Purse)

Name_____

Coat _____ Pants W-___L-____ Shirt _____ Belt _____

Shoes _____ Polo _____ Shorts _____ Und Wear _____

I PREFER

☐ Pleated Pants	☐ Plain Pants	☐ Cuffs
☐ Plain Bottoms	☐ 2 Button	☐ 3 Button
☐ Dbl Breast Suits	☐ Button Downs	☐ Str Coll.
☐ Spread Coll.	☐ O.T. Calf Socks	☐ Mid Calf Socks
☐ Conserv. Ties	☐ Mod. Conserv.	☐ No Preference

Comments: _____

Tim's Quick Reference Cut-Outs (His for Wallet)

e_____

_____ Pants W-___L-____ Shirt _____ Belt _____

s _____ Polo _____ Shorts _____ Und Wear _____

EFER

☐ Pleated Pants	☐ Plain Pants	☐ Cuffs
☐ Plain Bottoms	☐ 2 Button	☐ 3 Button
☐ Dbl Breast Suits	☐ Button Downs	☐ Str Coll.
☐ Spread Coll.	☐ O.T. Calf Socks	☐ Mid Calf Socks
☐ Conserv. Ties	☐ Mod. Conserv.	☐ No Preference

ments: _____

Tim's Quick Reference Cut-Outs (Hers for Purse)

Name_____

Coat _____ Pants W-___L-____ Shirt _____ Belt _____

Shoes _____ Polo _____ Shorts _____ Und Wear _____

I PREFER

☐ Pleated Pants	☐ Plain Pants	☐ Cuffs
☐ Plain Bottoms	☐ 2 Button	☐ 3 Button
☐ Dbl Breast Suits	☐ Button Downs	☐ Str Coll.
☐ Spread Coll.	☐ O.T. Calf Socks	☐ Mid Calf Socks
☐ Conserv. Ties	☐ Mod. Conserv.	☐ No Preference

Comments: _____

Appendix

The following pages contain abbreviations for Buying Records, Size Charts, Buying Histories, and a Glossary of Terms for use in compiling your own purchasing records. It is hoped these charts will be of value in helping you to better recognize and meet your clothing needs.

On a personal note, I would like to take this opportunity to thank you for buying SUIT YOURSELF. I hope you have enjoyed reading this book as much as I enjoyed writing it.

Tim Meehan

ABBREVIATIONS FOR BUYING RECORDS

	ABBREVIATION	EXAMPLES	DATE
C/P	SUIT (Coat & Pant)	2 C/P Char. Solid Navy Pin	
S/C	Sport Coat	1 S/C Herrbn.	
O/P	Pants (Odd Pants)	2 O/P Navy & Tan	
S	Shirts		
H	Hat		
B	Belt		
G	Gloves		
SS	Sport Shirt		
J	Jacket		
SW	Sweater		
SH	Shoes		
T	Tie		

When a suit or sport coat is old, or needs replacing, circle it and place an "R" at the end, as follows: (1 C/P Navy Pin) R.

In this way, you can still see what you have, what you need and what needs replacing.

Also, denote where purchases stop and start with dates: Example:

1) C/P Navy Pin. Blk B. Red T. Yellow T. -3/97
2) C/P Char. Solid & Olive Houndstooth - 6/97

ABBREVIATION GUIDE

SUIT
Yourself

A Practical Guide to Men's Attire
BY TIM MEEHAN

SIZE CHART

SIZE CHART FOR _____ DATE _____

ITEM	SIZE	ITEM	SIZE
SUIT/SPORT COAT		**PANT**	
SHIRT		**BELT**	
SPORT SHIRT		**SWEATER**	
HAT		**GLOVE**	
SHOE		**OUTERWEAR/JACKETS**	

ANNUAL BUDGET

Summer/Spring $ _____ Fall/Winter $ _____ Year _____

Summer/Spring $ _____ Fall/Winter $ _____ Year _____

Summer/Spring $ _____ Fall/Winter $ _____ Year _____

Summer/Spring $ _____ Fall/Winter $ _____ Year _____

Favorite colors, styles, etc.

_____

_____

Buying History

_____

_____

_____

_____

_____

SIZE CHART

SIZE CHART FOR _____ DATE _____

ITEM	SIZE	ITEM	SIZE
SUIT/SPORT COAT		PANT	
SHIRT		BELT	
SPORT SHIRT		SWEATER	
HAT		GLOVE	
SHOE		OUTERWEAR/JACKETS	

ANNUAL BUDGET

Summer/Spring $ _____ Fall/Winter $ _____ Year _____
Summer/Spring $ _____ Fall/Winter $ _____ Year _____
Summer/Spring $ _____ Fall/Winter $ _____ Year _____
Summer/Spring $ _____ Fall/Winter $ _____ Year _____

Favorite colors, styles, etc.

_____

_____

Buying History

_____

_____

_____

_____

_____

SIZE CHART

SIZE CHART FOR _____ DATE _____

ITEM	SIZE	ITEM	SIZE
SUIT/SPORT COAT		PANT	
SHIRT		BELT	
SPORT SHIRT		SWEATER	
HAT		GLOVE	
SHOE		OUTERWEAR/JACKETS	

ANNUAL BUDGET

Summer/Spring $ _____ Fall/Winter $ _____ Year _____
Summer/Spring $ _____ Fall/Winter $ _____ Year _____
Summer/Spring $ _____ Fall/Winter $ _____ Year _____
Summer/Spring $ _____ Fall/Winter $ _____ Year _____

Favorite colors, styles, etc.

_____

_____

Buying History

_____

_____

_____

_____

_____

SIZE CHART

SIZE CHART FOR _____ DATE _____

ITEM	SIZE	ITEM	SIZE
SUIT/SPORT COAT		PANT	
SHIRT		BELT	
SPORT SHIRT		SWEATER	
HAT		GLOVE	
SHOE		OUTERWEAR/JACKETS	

ANNUAL BUDGET

Summer/Spring $ _____ Fall/Winter $ _____ Year _____
Summer/Spring $ _____ Fall/Winter $ _____ Year _____
Summer/Spring $ _____ Fall/Winter $ _____ Year _____
Summer/Spring $ _____ Fall/Winter $ _____ Year _____

Favorite colors, styles, etc.

_____

_____

Buying History

_____

_____

_____

_____

_____

SIZE CHART

SIZE CHART FOR _____ DATE _____

ITEM	SIZE	ITEM	SIZE
SUIT/SPORT COAT		PANT	
SHIRT		BELT	
SPORT SHIRT		SWEATER	
HAT		GLOVE	
SHOE		OUTERWEAR/JACKETS	

ANNUAL BUDGET

Summer/Spring $ _____ Fall/Winter $ _____ Year _____
Summer/Spring $ _____ Fall/Winter $ _____ Year _____
Summer/Spring $ _____ Fall/Winter $ _____ Year _____
Summer/Spring $ _____ Fall/Winter $ _____ Year _____

Favorite colors, styles, etc.

_____

_____

Buying History

_____

_____

_____

_____

_____

SUIT
Yourself

A Practical Guide to Men's Attire
BY TIM MEEHAN

GLOSSARY OF TERMS

ACETATE: Textile fiber which is derived from a cellulose base often used in suit linings.

ALPACA: Fine Long fibers derived from a llama species that thrives in the Andes Mountains of Peru. Popular in sweaters, it has a soft feel and resilience.

ANGORA: A fiber derived from the long, silky hair of the Angora Goat.

ARGYLE: A multi-colored diamond design. Often used in hose, sweaters, and ties.

BALMORAL: Generally referred to as "bal." This is a laced shoe with a closed throat.

BARREL CUFF: A regular shirt cuff (one not requiring cuff links)

BASKET WEAVE: A weave that resembles the checkered pattern of a basket. It is noted for its lightness and airiness.

BATISTE: Sheer fabric or a plain weave closely related to madras in construction.

BERMUDAS: Knee-length walking shorts.

BESOM: A coat or jacket pocket having a stitched fold on the upper and lower sides.

BIRD'S EYE: A weave pattern producing a diamond-shaped design with a small dot that resembles a bird's eye.

BLAZER: A sport jacket usually in dark blue or other solid colors having metal buttons.

BLUCHER: A shoe style having two flaps on either side of the shoe tightened by eyelets and laces.

BOATER: Better known as a straw hat.

BOW TIE: A necktie tied around the neck area with two looped ends and two straight ends.

BOX PLEAT: A pleat with the edges folded in opposite directions: commonly used on shirts and jackets.

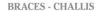

BRACES: Suspenders. (British Term)

BROADCLOTH: A very compact woven, elegant cloth with a velvet-like feel. Most often used in shirts and pajamas.

BROCADE: A rich jacquard-woven fabric that has interwoven designs of raised figures or flowers. Commonly used in neckware.

BROGUES: Heavy oxford shoes. Originally broguing meant detailing, such as perforations, pinking, or stitching.

BUCKSKIN: The tanned skins of antelope, deer, and elk. Usually dyed white or brown.

BUTTONDOWN COLLAR: A shirt collar where the points are fastened to the shirt with buttons and buttonholes.

CABLE STITCH: A type of raised stitch generally used on sweaters and socks that resembles a twisted rope.

CALFSKIN: Skin of a calf, very soft and durable; and used primarily to make gloves, shoes, and leather goods.

CAMEL HAIR: The soft undercoat of the double-hump camels of Outer Mongolia and China.

CARDIGAN: A collarless sweater that opens fully down the front. It is believed to have been designed by the 7th Earl of Cardigan. It is said he invented it as an extra layer of warmth while serving in the Crimean War.

CASHMERE: One of the finest and most luxurious fibers. It is taken from the Kashmir goats of Central Asia.

CAVALRY TWILL: A strong, rugged cloth having a raised cord on a 63-degree diagonal twill weave. Generally used for suits, slacks, and uniforms.

CHALK STRIPE: The broad vertical white stripes that resemble chalk lines. Commonly seen on Navy and Gray suits.

CHALLIS: Soft lightweight finely spun close woven worsted fabric. Commonly used for pajamas and neckwear.

SUIT
yourself

GLOSSARY OF TERMS

CHAMBRAY:	A fabric woven with colored warp and white filing producing a mottled colored surface with small plain-weave effect; usually used for shirts, sportswear, and pajamas.
CHAMOIS CLOTH:	A napped, sheared and dyed cotton fabric simulating chamois leather; used generally for jackets, gloves, and sportswear.
CHINO CLOTH:	An all cotton twill generally used in military uniforms and khaki trousers.
CORDOVAN:	Leather from the large muscle under the hide of a horse's buttocks. Completely smooth, having no surface grain also denotes the color of dark burgundy.
CORDUROY:	A durable heavy fabric with narrow or wide vertical ribs or wales.
COTTON:	The soft fiber from the seed pod of the cotton plant. The fibers are spun into yarn and thread for knitting and weaving. The majority of the world's crop is from the United States.
COVERT:	Fabric with very distinct diagonal twill. Having a mottled effect made by two-tone twist yarns, which are closely woven.
CREPE:	A fabric having a crinkled or pebbly type surface achieved by the use of tightly twisted yarns. Crepe can be woven in various weights.
CREW NECK:	A collarless opening, which follows the contour of the neck on shirts, sweaters, and underwear.
CUMMERBUND:	A waistband, having folds or pleats, which is worn over the top of the trousers with a dinner jacket or tuxedo.
CUT & SEWN:	Any article of apparel which is cut from fabric and then sewn by machine or hand.
DENIM:	A durable twill fabric woven with color warp (vertical threads) and white fill (horizontal threads).
DISTRICT CHECK:	A very uniform block pattern of plain squares.

DONEGAL: A woolen tweed fabric originally hand woven in Donegal, Ireland. Having thick, multicolor nubs woven in at random. A popular cloth for suits, sportswear and coats.

DROP: The number of inches the trouser size is from the suitcoat. For example a 40 regular suit, generally has a six inch trouser drop (a 34 waist).

END ON END: A weave with alternating horizontal yarns of white and color forming fine checks.

EPAULET: A strap on the shoulder of a coat, sport shirt or jacket. Having a military origin.

FELLING: A tailoring term meaning close stitching. Hand-felled means much of the final stitching on the collar, lapels, sleeves, and pockets, was done by hand.

FELT: A material produced from animal fibers by using steam moisture and pressure.

FILLING: Yarn running crosswise in a woven fabric.

FLANNEL: A loose woven fabric having a napped surface. Generally made of cotton or wool.

FLEECE: A luxurious fabric with a thick, deeply napped surface for warmth without weight. Can be a twill, plain weave or variations of either.

FOULARD: A twill weave, lightweight printed silk or rayon fabric; often used in neckwear, robes, mufflers, and handker chiefs.

FOUR-IN-HAND: This is the simplest of the neckwear knots to tie. The name comes from a coach being drawn by four horses in two teams, driven in tandem by a single person.

FRENCH CUFF: A shirt cuff requiring cuff links. Having double or turned back cuffs on the shirt.

GABARDINE: A very durable, firmly woven, 63 degree twill worsted fabric with a hard finish showing diagonal lines running from bottom left to top right on the fabric. Gabardine is most often used in suitings, sportswear, and outerwear.

GLOSSARY OF TERMS

GINGHAM:	A plain weave cotton fabric in checks, stripes or plaids. Generally used in sportswear.
GIRTH:	The circular all around measurement of a coat or jacket.
GLEN PLAID:	A pattern of small woven checks alternating with squares of large checks. Generally used in suits, sportswear and coats.
GORGE:	The seam on a coat where the collar meets the lapel.
GUN FLAP:	A styling detail on a trench coat. It is the extra layer of cloth across the shoulder.
HARRIS TWEED:	Fabric made of wool from the Outer Hebrides islands off the coast of Scotland. Having a certification mark used only on fabrics made from Scottish wool.
HERRINGBONE:	A broken twill weave pattern with a balanced zigzag design.
HOPSACK:	A coarse, loose basket-weave cloth made primarily with woolen yarns.
HOUNDS-TOOTH:	A woolen fabric having a small broken check pattern with a hook, resembling a dog's incisor. Generally used for suits, sportswear and coats in various weights.
INSEAM:	Measurement from crotch to bottom of trouser.
IRISH LINEN:	A fine lightweight linen woven from Irish flax. Used primarily for handkerchiefs and shirts.
JACQUARD:	A type of knitting that produces all-over or sectional designs of color and texture in a fabric.
LAMBSWOOL:	Usually refers to the first shearing of a lamb between 7-9 months of age. It is finer, and softer than wool from grown sheep.
LAPEL:	The portion of the front of the jacket that is turned back on both sides from the collar downward.
LINEN:	A rough fabric woven of flax. Generally used in suits, sport jackets, and sportswear.

LISLE: A fabric of fine, hard twisted, long staple cotton thread of two or more ply yarns: often used in hosiery, underwear, and sport shirts.

LONG STAPLE COTTON: Cotton fibers having a length not less that 1-1/8 inches.

MADDER: A type of vegetable dye stuff for fabrics; soft-tone prints for neckwear or sportswear; known as madder prints.

MADRAS: Cotton or spun rayon fabric having woven stripe checks or cord type patterns of same fabric color or contrast color.

MERINO: The wool from the Australian Merino sheep considered the most valuable wool produced in the world having softness, strength, and elasticity. Commonly used in suitings, sportcoats, and sportswear.

MOHAIR: The fleece of the Angora goat, having a soft and silky texture and a rich luster.

MONK-STRAP SHOE: A type of shoe having a strap across the instep and a buckle at the side.

NAILHEAD: A small dotted design used in suitings that resemble the heads of nails tightly grouped together.

NOTCHED LAPEL: A type of lapel in which the top line slants down in line with the collar seam.

NYLON: A strong synthetic fiber that can be washed and has elasticity often blended with natural fibers such as wool.

OXFORD CLOTH: A basketweave fabric of soft spun yarns having a thick warp and heavy fill yarns.

OXFORDS: Lace-up footwear that extends no higher than the ankle.

PAISLEY: A fabric of printed, woven designs with very colorful curved abstract figures. Paisley prints are often found on neckwear, mufflers, and sportswear.

PEAKED LAPEL: A type of lapel in which the top line slants up from the horizontal forming a peaking effect.

GLOSSARY OF TERMS

97

GLOSSARY OF TERMS

PINSTRIPES: Very fine stripes usually in white or gray found primarily on navy or gray suits.

PIMA COTTON: A fine grade long staple cross breed of Sea Island and Egyptian cotton grown in Pima County, Arizona.

PIQUE: Narrow wales, woven cotton fabric sometime made of rayon or silk. Wales run lengthwise or can form fine honeycomb or waffle weaves. Often used in shirts for formal wear.

PLAID: A pattern of unevenly spaced, box like stripes crossing at right angles. Originally each design distinguished a Scottish clan.

PLAIN WEAVE: The basic weave, in which each filling yarn passes over and under each successive warp yarn, alternating across each row.

POLYESTER: A man made fiber often blended with natural fiber in suits, sportcoats, slacks, and shirts, to resist wrinkles.

POPLIN: A durable plain-weave fabric resembling broadcloth but having a heavier rib. Most often used in suits, sports wear, and slacks.

PULLOVER: Sweater or shirt with or without sleeves having no front opening and must be pulled on over the head.

RAGLAN: A sleeve that extends to the neckline with slanted seams from the underarm to the neck for a free-swinging movement.

RAMIE: Is a natural fiber derived from the ramie plant. It is similar in nature and physical properties to flax, from which linen is spun.

REGIMENTAL STRIPES: Striped ties having the colors and striping patterns of British army regiments.

REP (REPP): A distinct heavy crosswise ribbed fabric with a soft luster. Used commonly for men's coats and neckwear.

REVERSE PLEAT: Pleats that face outward from the zipper.

RISE: The distance form the crotch to the top of the waistband in trousers.

SAXONY: A lightweight wool fabric with a slightly napped surface originally describing wool grown in Saxony Germany.

SEERSUCKER: A crinkly, lightweight cotton fabric. Popular in suits and sportswear for summer garments. Originally from India.

SEA ISLAND: A type of cotton grown on islands off the coasts of South Carolina, Georgia, and Florida, as well as the West Indies.

SHARKSKIN: A smooth finished twill weave fabric used in wool for suits and silk for ties.

SHAWL COLLAR: Long rolling unnotched lapel. Commonly used on tuxedo jackets, dinner jackets, and robes.

SHETLAND: A medium-textured, coarse, warm fabric with a raised finish, made from wool grown on the Shetland Islands of Scotland. Generally used for sportswear, coats, and knitwear.

SILK: Natural fiber from the cocoon of the silkworm, it is resilient and has a lustrous hand.

SIZING: A finishing process to add strength and smoothness, stiffness and weight to yarn or fabric.

STAPLE: A term describing the average length of a fiber also refers to a basic in clothing.

SUEDE: Leather having a napped surface, used in casual shoes. It is also used in leather goods and some clothing.

SUSPENDERS: Two bands or straps worn over the shoulders and across the back attaching at the trousers for support.

TAB COLLAR: Shirt collar, held in place by snaps or button tabs.

TARTAN: A plaid design specific to Scottish Clans.

TATTERSALL: A very uniform square pattern of lines of two or more colors forming squares on a solid background.

TICKET POCKET: A small pocket located at the waist above the regular pocket on the right side of a jacket or coat.

GLOSSARY OF TERMS

TROPICAL WORSTED:	A lightweight worsted cloth woven from fine yarns mainly in plain weave. These clear finished fabrics are used for warm weather suits and sportswear.
TURTLENECK SWEATER:	A knitted garment with a turned over collar, usually ribbed without a front opening covering the neck.
TWEED:	A pure wool, durable with a rough surface appearance and pliable yet firm in the weave. Tweeds can be produced in various weights and patterns for suits, sportswear and coats.
TWILL:	The second basic weave. Shows a distinct diagonal line that runs from bottom left to top right on face of the fabric.
TWIST:	A yarn formed by twisting two or more strands together.
V-NECK:	A neckline which reaches a V point on front.
VELOUR:	A close, thick-bodied, evenly napped woolen fabric with a soft hand and velvet appearance.
VENETIAN CLOTH:	A medium-to-heavyweight worsted covert fabric with a lustrous finish. Generally used for suits, sportswear, coats and linings.
VENT:	Slit in the back center bottom, or sides of a jacket or coat.
VICUNA:	Wool from the fine undercoat of the vicuna goats of the Andes in South America. Having a very fine, and soft hand.
VIRGIN WOOL:	Natural wool being used for the first time in a fabric.
WARP:	The vertical yarns of a woven fabric, to which the filling yarns are added.
WEAVING:	A process of forming fabric on a loom by interlacing warp and filling threads with each other.
WEIGHT:	The weight in ounces of a linear yard of fabric.

SUIT *Yourself*

WELT: A small cord covered with fabric and sewn on a seam or border for strength. Also a raised double edge, strip, insert, or seam for ornament or reinforcement.

WHIPCORD: A twill fabric with distinct diagonal cords that run from bottom left to upper right. It is similar to but coarser than gabardine.

WINDSOR COLLAR: A shirt collar with a wide spread between the collar points.

WINDOWPANE CHECK: Large squares of a third color over the two squares of a smaller check, creating a box over-plaid pattern. Used in suits, sportswear and outerwear.

WING-TIP SHOE: Type of shoe distinguished by the tip having perforations in the shape of the spread wings of a bird.

WOOL: Wool-bearing sheep are raised in almost every country of the world. There are literally hundreds of varieties and breeds, making for a wide range of fiber types, from ultra-soft to crisp, thus making wool one of the most versatile of the animal fibers.

WORSTED: A smooth, compact yarn spun from long wool fibers.

YARN: Continuous strands of spun fiber, cleaned drawn and twisted. Made of silk, wool, linen, cotton or manmade fibers.

ZEPHYR WOOL YARN: A very fine, lightweight worsted wool yarn, made from the finest virgin wool grades.

GLOSSARY OF TERMS